Written by
Kimberly Jordano and Kim Adsit

Editor: Kim Cernek
Illustrator: Linda Weller
Cover Illustrator: David Christensen
Designer/Production: Moonhee Pak/Cari Helstrom
Cover Designer: Barbara Peterson
Art Director: Tom Cochrane
Project Director: Stephanie Oberc

Table of Contents

Introduction

Journal writing is an easy way to collect ideas, thoughts, and responses written by children. The hard part is keeping children motivated to do their best work and teaching them how to write effectively. *Jumping into Journals* gives you dozens of ideas for captivating children's interest in writing and suggestions for developing their writing skills.

The purpose of journal writing with emergent and beginning readers is to teach them the concepts of print and basic writing skills. Children are encouraged to manipulate sounds and letters in order to print the words that express their *schema*, or what they know.

Journal writing is effective for children at all levels of literacy development because they are encouraged to write about their own experiences. As children write the stories of their lives on paper, they become interested in sharing their work with others. This sharing time inspires children to read and write more and more.

Jumping into Journals helps you incorporate the benefits of journal writing into every aspect of your curriculum. You will find simple directions for making a dozen unique cross-curricular journals. There are also practical ideas for managing journal writing time and tips for conferencing, publishing, and keeping children motivated to do their best work.

Jumping into Journals is a comprehensive approach to journal writing. The varied ideas in this resource will help you develop and maintain a classroom routine that emphasizes how much fun it is to write.

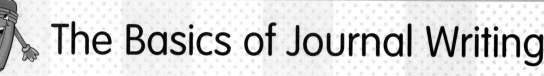

The Basics of Journal Writing

Why Is Journal Writing Beneficial?

Journal writing promotes authentic writing. In journals, children are encouraged to write about their experiences or their response to something they have seen, heard, felt, or imagined. Children feel comfortable writing about personal topics and gain confidence when they do.

Journal writing also presents a terrific opportunity to model writing skills. The minilessons in *Jumping into Journals* help children become better writers as they learn to: apply phonics skills; brainstorm and organize ideas; use punctuation; develop focused, detailed writing; follow spelling rules; incorporate letter and word spacing; form letters; and write in complete sentences.

Who Is Capable of Journal Writing?

The youngest learners will enjoy and benefit from journal writing. Emergent writers move through three stages of writing. First, a child puts meaning on paper in the form of a drawing. Over time, a child creates meaning by combining pictures and text. Finally, a child writes meaningful text independent of pictures.

What Are the Components of Journal Writing?

Journal writing is most successful when the following four components are included: modeled minilessons, actual writing, conferencing, and sharing. *Jumping into Journals* shows you how to seamlessly incorporate all four elements into your regular writing program.

When Do Children Write in Journals?

Try introducing journal writing into one or all of the following parts of your learning day:

- As soon as children have settled into their seats first thing in the morning
- To have children record the work they have done at a center
- To have children record their thoughts about their math, science, and social studies lessons

How Are Journals Made and Managed?

Journals are very simple to construct. Fold several pieces of unlined or lined paper together under a construction paper cover, and staple the book at the crease. You could also insert paper into a three-ring binder or a three-prong pocket folder to make journals that can be expanded over time. Encourage children to decorate the covers of their journals, or have them use the reproducible covers in this resource.

Give each child a rectangular magazine container. Photograph each child, and attach his or her photo and name to the front of the container. Encourage children to store their journals in this personalized box.

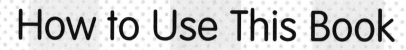

How to Use This Book

Before you begin using journals in your classroom, help children make the "tools" they will need to develop as a writer. A handy Word Wall list, a sheet featuring the sounds of the alphabet, and a list of favorite words are just a few of the tools (see pages 7–10) that will help children expand their vocabulary. Help each child make a My Writing Toolbox (see page 7) to store these tools that will help them write better journals. Encourage children to keep their "toolbox" close whenever they write.

Then choose a type of journal to introduce, such as the Literature Journal or Math Journal. Copy the reproducible pages, and follow the simple directions to make an eye-catching journal for each child in your class. Use the featured thematic minilesson and coordinating reproducible pages or graphic organizer to teach children how to write an authentic entry in their journal. Conference with each child about his or her writing, and attach a thematic Award Ticket to children's work to motivate them to continue to do their best journal writing.

Tools for Journal Writing

The following "tools" will help children organize and transport everything they need to successfully write in their journals. Children will have sight words, classmates' names, and other useful information at their fingertips.

Materials

- My Writing Toolbox reproducible (page 11)
- glue
- two-pocket folder

My Writing Toolbox

Make a copy of the My Writing Toolbox reproducible for each child, and glue each copy onto a separate folder. Write each child's name on the front of his or her folder. Tell children to store the other tools for writing that they will receive in this folder.

Materials

- Traveling Word Wall reproducible (page 12)
- Alphabet Grid reproducible (pages 13–14)
- glue
- file folders

Traveling Word Wall

Make a copy of the Traveling Word Wall and Alphabet Grid reproducibles for each child. For each child, glue the Traveling Word Wall title page to the front of a file folder. Glue both pages of the Alphabet Grid to the inside of the folder. Write the child's name on the front of his or her folder. Give children their folder, and encourage them to insert their Traveling Word Wall into their My Writing Toolbox folder (see above). Tell children they will write new sight words that they learn on this Word Wall list.

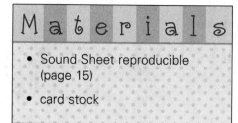

Materials

- Sound Sheet reproducible (page 15)
- card stock

Sound Sheet

Make an enlarged copy of the Sound Sheet reproducible, and display it in the classroom. Make a copy of the Sound Sheet reproducible on card stock for each child. Tell children to insert this reproducible in their My Writing Toolbox folder (see page 7). Tell children to use their Sound Sheet whenever they need help with a new letter. For example, if a child asks what a *b* looks like, you can tell him or her to find the letter that is beneath the book.

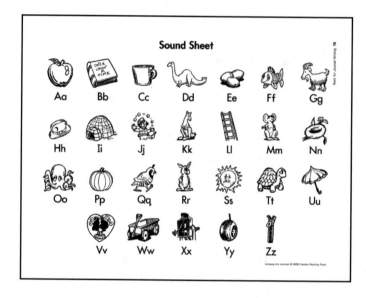

Materials

- Nifty Name Wall reproducible (page 16)
- digital camera
- scissors
- glue
- marker

Nifty Name Wall

Take each child's picture with a digital camera, and print the photographs. Cut out each child's face. Make several copies of the Nifty Name Wall reproducible. Invite children to help you arrange the photos in alphabetical order by first name. Glue one face to each oval. Write the first name of each child below his or her picture. Make enlarged copies of the finished Nifty Name Wall reproducibles, and display them in the classroom. Make copies of the finished Nifty Name Wall reproducibles for each child, and have each child put the copies in his or her My Writing Toolbox folder (see page 7). Encourage children to look at the names on these papers when they need to spell the name of a classmate.

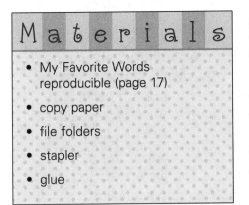

Materials

- My Favorite Words reproducible (page 17)
- copy paper
- file folders
- stapler
- glue

My Favorite Words Folder

Give each child seven pieces of paper. Show children how to place one piece of paper over another so that a ½" (1.25 cm) margin appears at the bottom. Have children place another piece over the top piece, leaving a ½" margin at the bottom again, and so on until they have used all seven pieces. Tell them to hold their papers securely in place and then fold the top piece of paper over so that a ½" margin appears at the bottom. Tell children to repeat this with the remaining pieces of paper. Give each child a a file folder. Have children open their folders and place their papers on one side. Help children staple their papers to their folder along the top. Give children seven additional pieces of paper, and have them make another "step book" to staple to the other side of their folder.

Have children write the uppercase and lowercase letters from *A* to *M* along the left margin of the "steps" on the left-hand side of their folder. Ask children to write the letters from *N* to *Z* along the left margin of the "steps" on the right-hand side of their folder. Explain to children that they will write their favorite words on the step with the matching first letter. As an option, have children draw a small picture to help them remember their favorite words. Give children a My Favorite Words reproducible to glue to the cover of their folder. Invite children to write their name on the cover of their folder. Then tell children to place their folder in their My Writing Toolbox folder (see page 7).

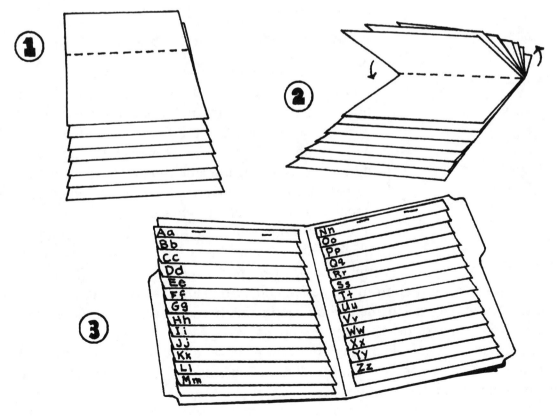

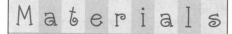

Alphabox Grid

Make 13 copies of the Alphabox Grid reproducible on colored paper. Write the uppercase and lowercase version of each letter in the top left corner of each square. Arrange the papers in alphabetical order, and staple them to a board.

Invite children to select their favorite words from the stories you have read together. Write each word on a sticky note, and invite children to place each word on a line in the "alphabox" with the matching first letter. Once you have completed a unit of study, remove all of the sticky notes from the board, and ask children to decide on their five favorite words. Tell children to add these five words to their My Favorite Words folder (see page 9).

Alphabox Grid

A a	and after	B b	big before best
		bear	

Making Space for the "Space"man

- "Space"man reproducible (page 19)
- card stock
- scissors
- self-adhesive laminating sheets
- adhesive putty
- marker
- chart paper

Make three enlarged copies of the "Space"man reproducible on card stock, cut out the "space"men figures, and laminate them. Place some putty on the back of each cutout. Use the "space"men to show children how to leave spaces between the words they write. Give several children a "space"man cutout. Write the first word of a sentence on chart paper, and invite a child to place a "space"man after it. Write another word, and have a different child place another "space"man after that word. Continue until you have written several sentences. Then remove the "space"men from the paper, and emphasize the spaces that "appear." Use the "space"men when conducting modeled writing, daily news, interactive writing, or other group writing activities. Make one copy of the "Space"man reproducible on card stock for each child to cut apart. Tell children to place the "space"men in their My Writing Toolbox folder (see page 7) for use when necessary in daily writing.

My Writing Toolbox

Name _____

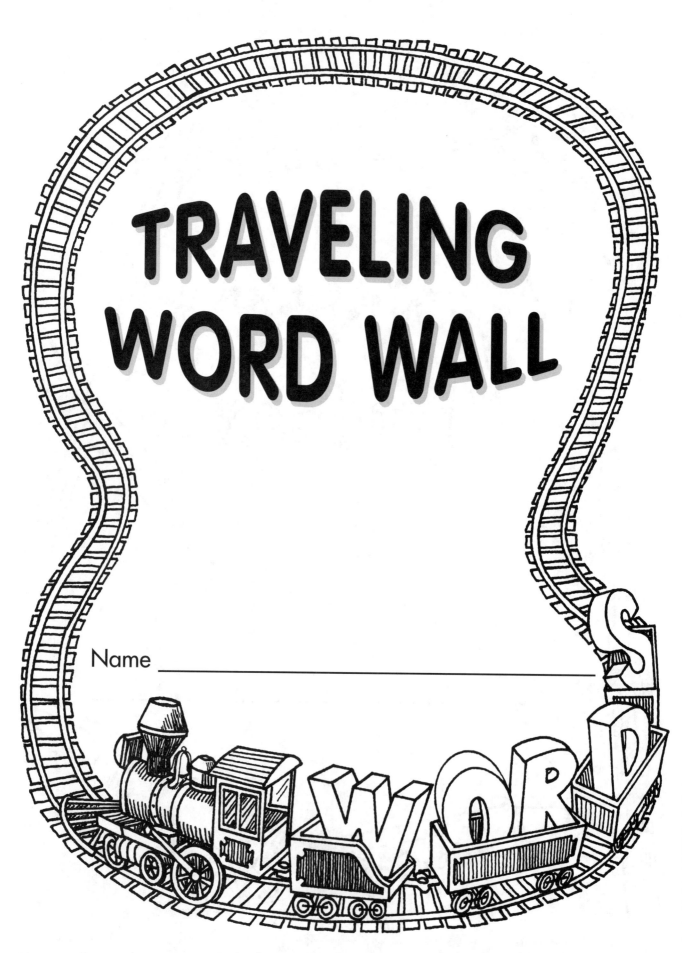

TRAVELING WORD WALL

Name _____

Alphabet Grid

Aa	Bb	Cc	Dd	Ee	Ff	Gg
Hh	Ii	Jj	Kk	Ll	Mm	Nn

Alphabet Grid

Oo	Pp	Qq	Rr	Ss	Tt	Uu

Vv	Ww	Xx	Yy	Zz

Sound Sheet

Aa

Bb

Cc

Dd

Ee

Ff

Gg

Hh

Ii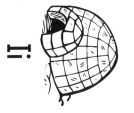

Jj

Kk

Ll

Mm

Nn

Oo

Pp

Qq

Rr

Ss

Tt

Uu

Vv

Ww

Xx

Yy

Zz

Jumping into Journals © 2006 Creative Teaching Press

Nifty Name Wall

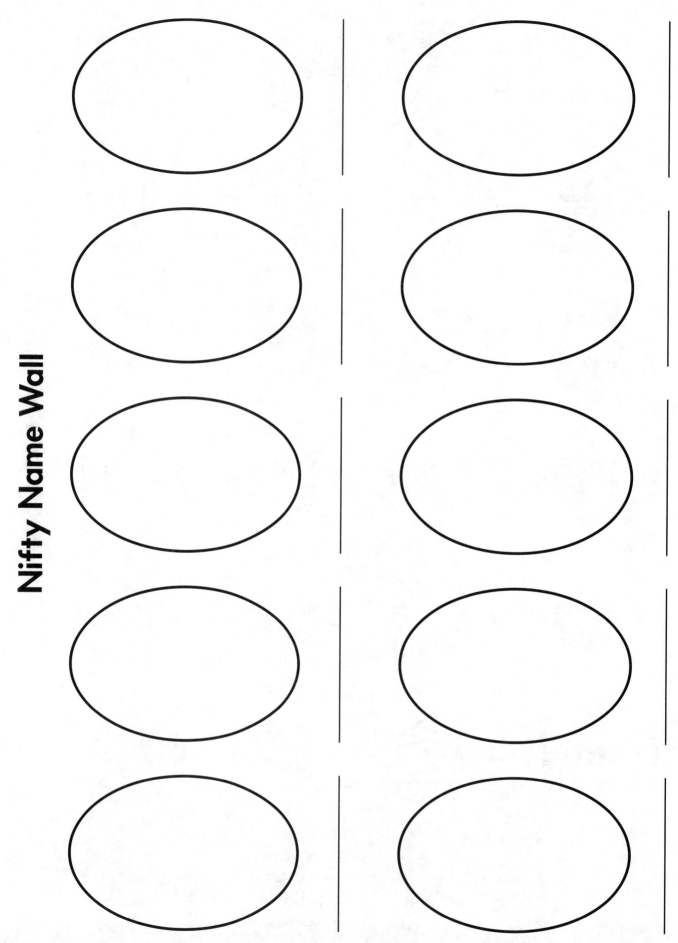

My Favorite Words

Name _____

Alphabox Grid

"Space" man

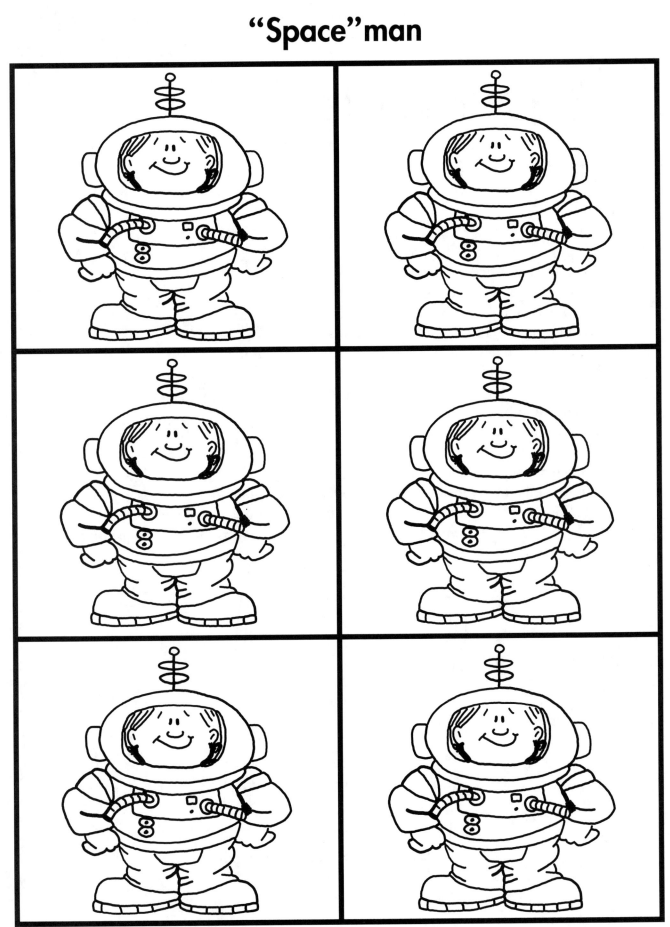

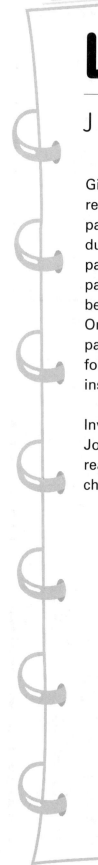

Literature

J O U R N A L

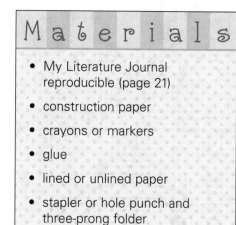

Give each child a My Literature Journal reproducible and a piece of construction paper. Invite children to color their reproducible and glue it to their construction paper. Give children several pieces of paper. Help children staple their papers behind their construction paper cover. Or tell children to glue their construction paper cover to the front of a three-prong folder, and help them hole-punch and insert their papers inside.

Materials

- My Literature Journal reproducible (page 21)
- construction paper
- crayons or markers
- glue
- lined or unlined paper
- stapler or hole punch and three-prong folder

Invite children to write in their Literature Journal their response to a read-aloud, a shared-reading activity, or a guided-reading selection. Encourage children to write about story elements (e.g., characters, setting) or about their own experience with the topic of the story.

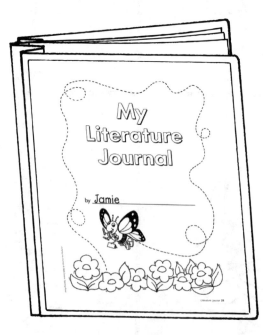

My Literature Journal

by _____

Are You My Mother?

1. Read aloud *Are You My Mother?* by P. D. Eastman. Discuss with children the different animals and objects the little bird encounters in its search for its mother. Tell children you are going to write a journal entry about the part of the story where the bird discovers his home is a nest in a tree. Model for children how to write the date at the top of the page, and remind them to begin writing on the left side of the page.

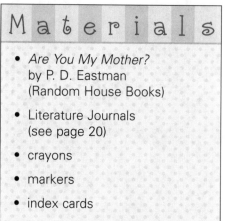

Materials

- *Are You My Mother?* by P. D. Eastman (Random House Books)
- Literature Journals (see page 20)
- crayons
- markers
- index cards

2. Draw a tree, a bird, and a nest in your journal, and invite children to draw similar ones in their journals. Talk about what you are thinking as you draw. Point to the tree on your page, and ask children to identify the beginning sound. Write a *t* beside the tree. Repeat the procedure with the bird and the nest. Ask children to write the same letters in their Literature Journals. Challenge children to write additional letters for each word if they are ready.

3. Write *This*, *is*, and *the* on separate index cards, and display them on a board or a chart. Help children practice reading the words.

4. Revisit the illustrations of the tree, bird, and nest and the corresponding letters. Then, review the sight words (i.e., *This*, *is*, and *the*). Tell children they are now ready to write a sentence. Model for children how to write *This is the* **t**. Point out the uppercase letter at the beginning of the sentence, the spaces between the words, and the ending punctuation. Ask children to read the sentence back to you. Encourage children to help you write a similar sentence for the bird and the nest. Invite children to write all three sentences in their journals. Encourage children to practice reading their sentences to each other.

This is the t.

This is the b.

This is the n.

Award Tickets

Copy and cut apart this page. Attach one "ticket" to an entry in each child's Literature Journal.

This award goes to

_____

for retelling the story

_____

so well!

Bravo! You are quite a bookworm!

This award goes to

_____

for retelling the story

_____

so well!

Bravo! You are quite a bookworm!

This award goes to

_____

for retelling the story

_____

so well!

Bravo! You are quite a bookworm!

This award goes to

_____

for retelling the story

_____

so well!

Bravo! You are quite a bookworm!

Alphabet
J O U R N A L

Give each child an Alphabet Journal reproducible and a piece of construction paper. Invite children to color their reproducible and glue it to their piece of construction paper. Give children a set of Alphabet reproducibles and 26 pieces of paper. Have children cut out each pair of uppercase and lowercase letters, and tell them to glue one pair to each piece of copy paper. Help children staple their papers behind their construction paper cover. Or tell children to glue their construction paper cover to the front of a three-prong folder, and help them hole-punch and insert their letter papers inside.

Introduce a letter, and invite children to draw pictures, list words, or write sentences on their journal page that correspond with the letter. As an option, have children attach stickers or glue other small items that have a matching first letter on their pages.

M a t e r i a l s

- Alphabet Journal reproducible (page 25)
- Alphabet reproducibles (pages 26–28)
- construction paper
- crayons or markers
- glue
- copy paper
- scissors
- stapler or hole punch and three-prong folders
- stickers or small items (optional)

_____'s

Alphabet Journal

ABCDEFG...
Come along and
learn letters with me!

Alphabet

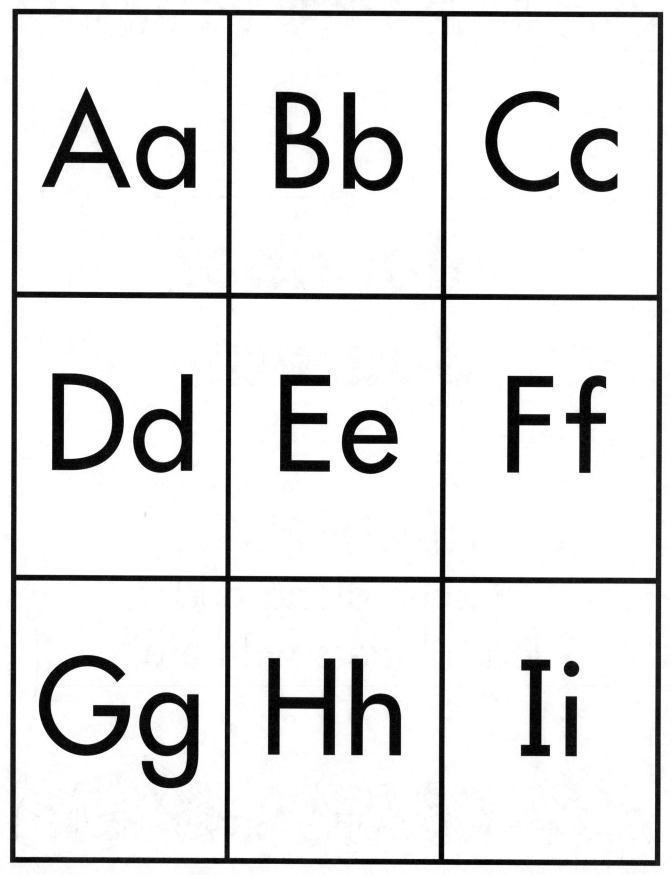

Alphabet

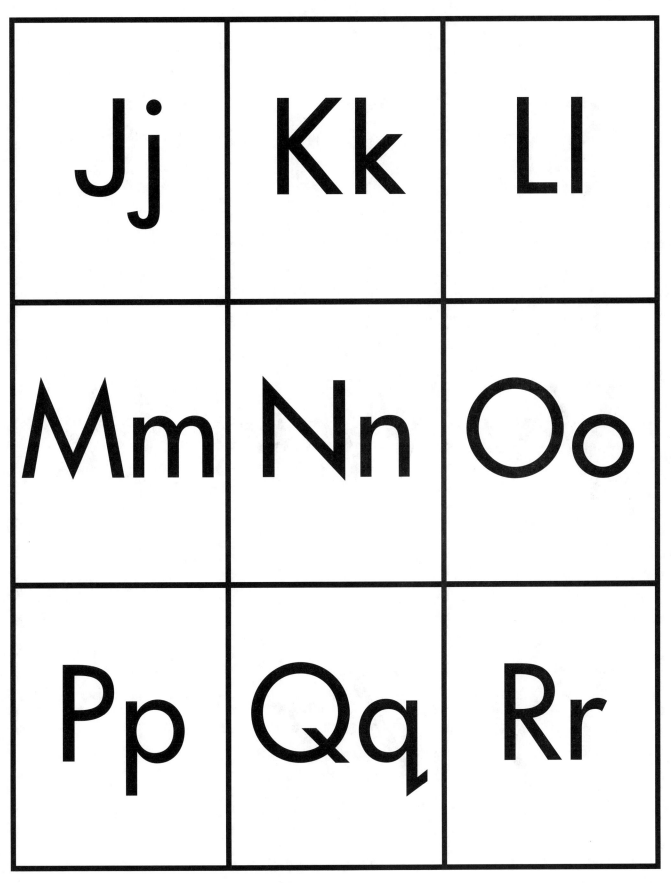

Jj	Kk	Ll
Mm	Nn	Oo
Pp	Qq	Rr

Alphabet

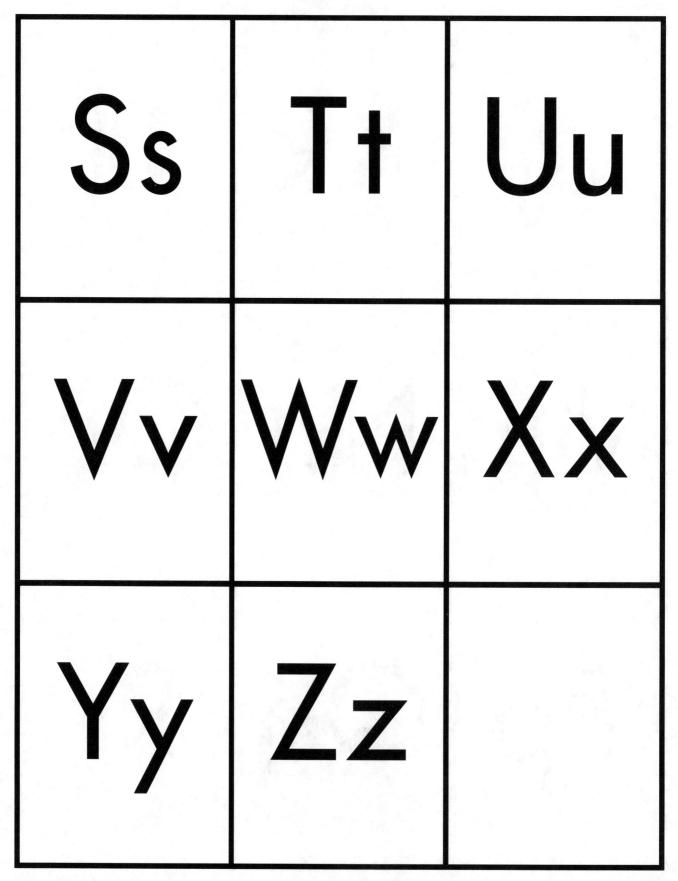

S s	T t	U u
V v	W w	X x
Y y	Z z	

Word Sorts

1. Write a letter (e.g., *c*) at the top of a piece of chart paper. Tell children that they are going to think of words that begin with that letter.

2. Invite children to brainstorm a list of words that begin with the target letter. Encourage children to name as many words as they can, and write the words on the chart paper.

3. Show children Pictionary entries, picture cards, and toys (e.g., car, cat, camera, and crayon) that begin with the target letter to help children name additional words.

4. Cut apart the words on the list, and invite children to help you sort them by one attribute. Words could be sorted by the number of letters or syllables or by ending sounds.

5. Cut out from butcher paper the shape of the target letter, and invite children to glue the words on it.

6. Invite children to write some of the words in their Alphabet Journal on the corresponding letter page.

Materials

- Alphabet Journals (see page 24)
- chart paper
- marker
- Pictionary
- picture cards
- toys with the same beginning sound
- scissors
- butcher paper
- glue

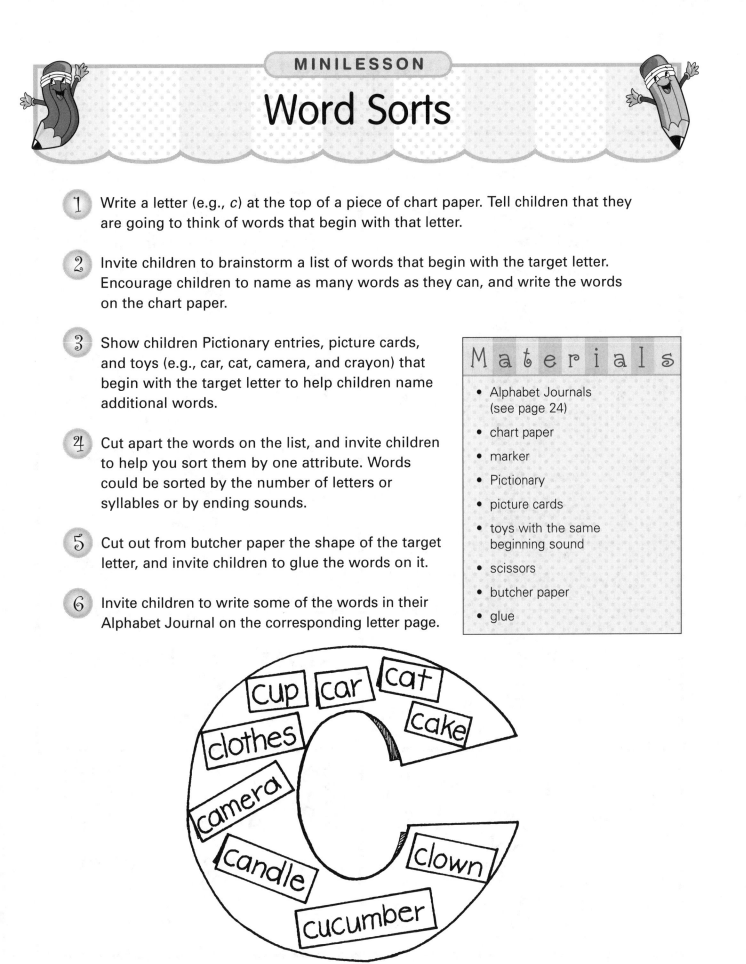

Award Tickets

Copy and cut apart this page. Attach one "ticket" to an entry in each child's Alphabet Journal.

Word Families

J O U R N A L

Make several copies of the My Word Families reproducible, and cut the pages in half to make a cover for each child's journal. Cut several sheets of construction paper in half. Give each child a reproducible and half a piece of construction paper. Invite children to color their reproducible and glue it to their construction paper. Make several copies of the Word Family reproducible, and cut them apart. Give each child a pile of Word Family papers, and tell children to place their cover on top. Help children bind their journal.

Use magnetic, foam, or wooden letters to make a word-family word (e.g., *cake*, *top*, or *jump*). Give a set of letters to each child, and invite children to form the same word. Tell children to write the word on the first page of their Word Families Journal. Show children how to change the onset (i.e., the first letter) to make a new word. Ask children to make new words and list them in their journal. Encourage children to use this journal to help them spell words as they write.

Materials

- My Word Families reproducible (page 32)
- Word Family reproducible (page 33)
- scissors
- construction paper
- crayons or markers
- glue
- bookbinding materials (e.g., stapler, hole punch/ curling ribbon)
- letter manipulatives (e.g., magnetic, foam, wooden)

My Word Families

Name _____

My Word Families

Name _____

Word Family

Stacking Up New Words

1. Write rimes (e.g., *-ake*, *-op*, or *-ump*) on separate square blocks. Write various onsets (e.g., *c*, *t*, or *j*) on separate rectangular blocks.

2. Arrange the blocks to show *c* and *-ake*. Invite children to help you sound out /c/ and /āk/ to make *cake*. Write *cake* in a Word Families Journal, and have children write the same word in their journal.

3. Change the *c* to *t*, and ask children to sound out the /t/ and /āk/ to make *take*. Write *take* in a Word Families Journal, and have children write the same word in their journal.

4. Continue changing onsets and rimes to make new words. Write each new word in a Word Families Journal, and have children write the same words in their journal. Remind children to write the date at the top of their journal entry.

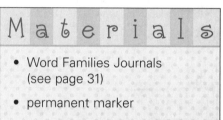

Materials

- Word Families Journals (see page 31)
- permanent marker
- blocks (square, rectangular)

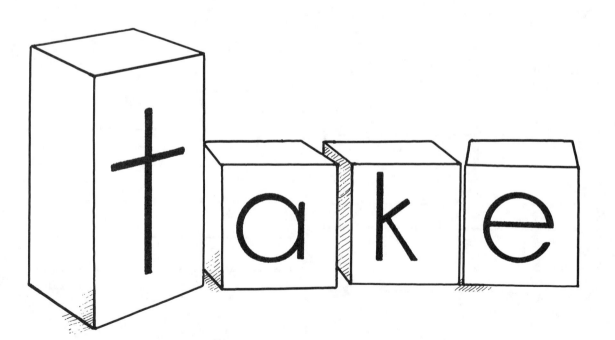

Award Tickets

Copy and cut apart this page. Attach one "ticket" to an entry in each child's Word Families Journal.

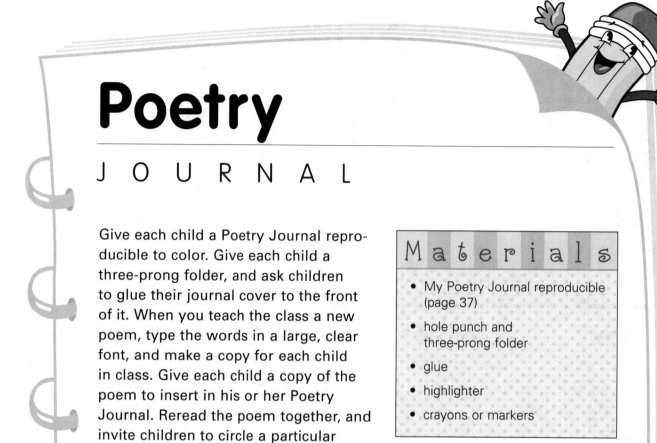

Poetry

J O U R N A L

Give each child a Poetry Journal reproducible to color. Give each child a three-prong folder, and ask children to glue their journal cover to the front of it. When you teach the class a new poem, type the words in a large, clear font, and make a copy for each child in class. Give each child a copy of the poem to insert in his or her Poetry Journal. Reread the poem together, and invite children to circle a particular letter and/or underline familiar sight words. Invite children to use a highlighter to identify punctuation marks. Encourage children to draw a picture beside the poem.

Materials

- My Poetry Journal reproducible (page 37)
- hole punch and three-prong folder
- glue
- highlighter
- crayons or markers

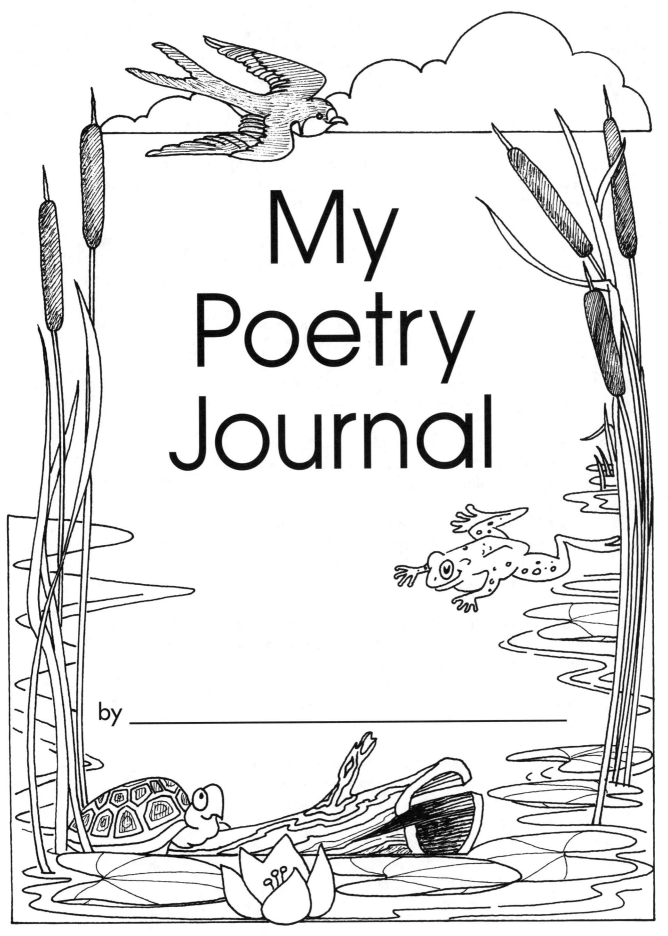

My Poetry Journal

by _____

"Little Bear"

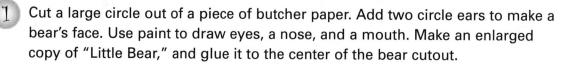
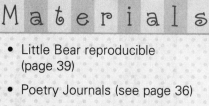

1. Cut a large circle out of a piece of butcher paper. Add two circle ears to make a bear's face. Use paint to draw eyes, a nose, and a mouth. Make an enlarged copy of "Little Bear," and glue it to the center of the bear cutout.

2. Recite for children "Little Bear." Repeat the poem, and encourage children to join you until they know it well.

3. Make a transparency copy of the Little Bear reproducible, and display it on an overhead projector. Read the poem, and point to each word you read. Ask children to find the rhyming words, and use a green marker to draw a box around them.

4. Give a child a pointer, and ask him or her to point to each *b* he or she sees. Use a red marker to circle each *b* on the transparency.

5. Give a different child the pointer, and ask him or her to point to any *-y* ending he or she sees. Use a blue marker to underline the *-y* ending on the transparency.

6. Give the pointer to a different child, and ask him or her to point to each punctuation mark he or she sees. Use a yellow marker to highlight each punctuation mark on the transparency.

7. Review with children why you made the green, red, blue, and yellow marks.

8. Give each child a copy of the Little Bear reproducible. Have children use colored pencils or markers to make the same marks on their paper that you made on the transparency.

9. Invite children to color their poetry page. Help children hole-punch their papers and insert them into their Poetry Journal.

Materials

- Little Bear reproducible (page 39)
- Poetry Journals (see page 36)
- scissors
- colored butcher paper
- paint
- glue
- transparency/overhead projector
- transparency markers (green, red, blue, yellow)
- pointer
- colored pencils or markers
- hole punch

Little Bear

Little Bear,
Little Bear,
As hungry as can be.
Will you please
Share a snack
With little ole me?

Little Bear

Little Bear,

Little Bear,

As hungry as can be.

Will you please

Share a snack

With little ole me?

Award Tickets

Copy and cut apart this page. Attach one "ticket" to an entry in each child's Poetry Journal.

Math

J O U R N A L

Give each child a My Math Journal reproducible and several pieces of construction paper. Tell children to arrange their construction paper in a pile and place it in a landscape position on their desk. Help children hole-punch several holes along one side of the papers and use curling ribbon to bind the book together. Invite children to color their journal reproducible and glue it to the top piece of construction paper.

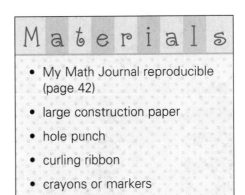

Materials

- My Math Journal reproducible (page 42)
- large construction paper
- hole punch
- curling ribbon
- crayons or markers
- glue

Use Math Journals to help children practice writing numbers, arranging numbers in order, drawing and labeling shapes, making patterns, comparing more or less, telling time, adding, or solving story problems. Or give children a simple math-related art project to complete on a page of their Math Journal, and encourage them to write about their project. Try one of the following activities:

- Have children make fruit or vegetable print patterns in two different colors. Ask children to label their pattern (e.g., AB, AABB).

- Invite children to glue cotton balls on a page to make two snowmen. Have children write about which snowman has more "snow" and which has less.

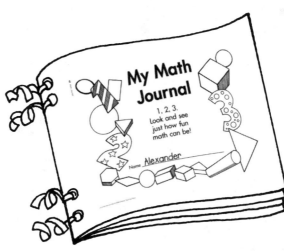

My Math Journal

1, 2, 3.
Look and see
just how fun
math can be!

Name _____

Fall Leaves Are Falling!

1. Copy the Tree Trunk reproducible on brown construction paper, and give one to each child to cut out. Invite children to glue it to a page of their Math Journal.

2. Invite children to tear a combination of ten "leaves" from colored construction paper. Tell children to glue some of the leaves on the "tree" and the remaining leaves on the "ground."

3. Make several copies of the Fall Leaves Are Falling! reproducible. Cut apart the strips, and give one to each child. Tell children to glue their paper strip to the bottom of their paper.

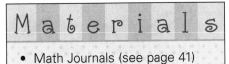

Materials

- Math Journals (see page 41)
- Tree Trunk reproducible (page 44)
- Fall Leaves Are Falling! reproducible (page 45)
- construction paper (brown, yellow, orange, red, green)
- scissors
- glue

4. Tell children to write their name on the first blank line. Encourage children to count the number of leaves on their tree, and have them write the number on the second blank line. Ask children to count the number of leaves below their tree, and have them write the number on the third blank line.

5. Encourage children to read aloud their complete sentences to each other. Remind children to write the date at the top of their journal page.

Vince sees fall leaves all around. 6 are on the tree, and 4 are on the ground.

Tree Trunk

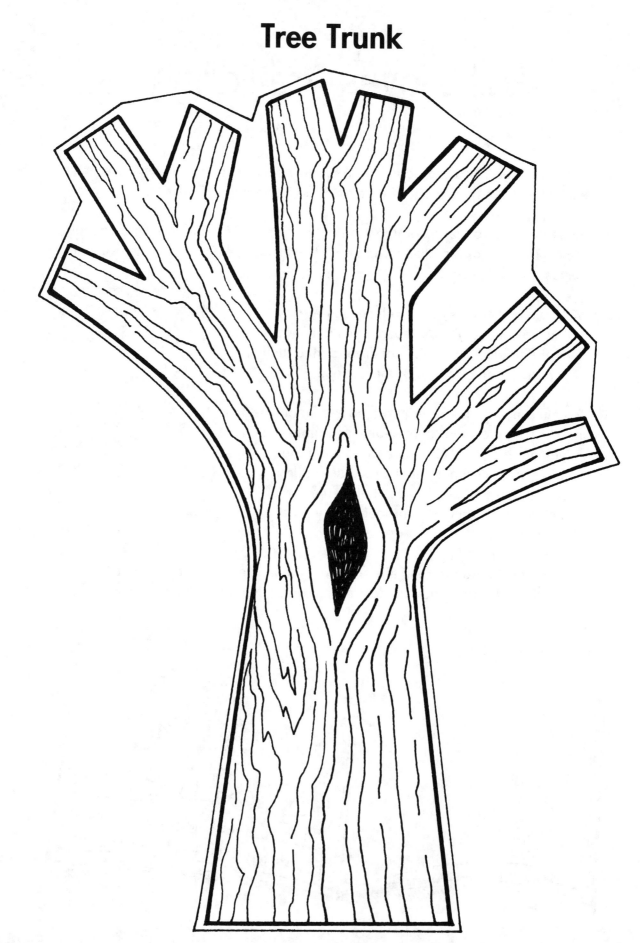

Fall Leaves Are Falling!

_____ sees fall leaves all around.

_____ are on the tree, and _____ are on the ground!

_____ sees fall leaves all around.

_____ are on the tree, and _____ are on the ground!

_____ sees fall leaves all around.

_____ are on the tree, and _____ are on the ground!

Award Tickets

Copy and cut apart this page. Attach one "ticket" to an entry in each child's Math Journal.

Zero-the-Hero

J O U R N A L

Assemble special math journals that are solely dedicated to "Zero-the-Hero." Make a copy of the Zero-the-Hero Journal reproducible for each child. Give each child a Zero-the-Hero reproducible and a piece of construction paper. Invite children to color their reproducible and glue it to their piece of construction paper. Give each child 18 Zero's Surprise reproducibles, and help children staple the papers behind their construction paper cover. Or tell children to glue their construction paper cover to the front of a three-prong folder, and help them hole-punch and insert their papers inside.

Materials

- Zero-the-Hero Journal reproducible (page 48)
- Zero's Surprise reproducible (page 49)
- construction paper
- crayons or markers
- glue
- stapler or hole punch and three-prong folder
- O-shaped treats or toys
- paper lunch sack

Arrange for "Zero-the-Hero" to leave O-shaped treats or toys in a paper lunch sack in your classroom every ten days of school. Insert a different number of items each time, and label the paper lunch sack with the number that represents how many days the children have been in school. Invite children to count, sort, and/or make a pattern with the items in the sack. Encourage children to try to fairly divide between them the number of items in the sack. Ask children to write about what they have counted and sorted in their Zero-the-Hero Journals.

_____'s

Zero-the-Hero Journal

ZERO, YOU'RE A HERO!

100
50
40
90
70
60
30
20
80
10

10, 20, 30. I can count by tens.
40, 50, 60. Let's count again.
70, 80, 90. We're almost done.
100! Wasn't that fun?

Jumping into Journals © 2006 Creative Teaching Press

Zero's Surprise

Today is the _____ day of school.

Zero-the-Hero brought _____

_____

_____

_____.

Zero-the-Hero's Guessing Game

1. On the tenth day of school, write *10* on a paper lunch sack, and fill it with 25 to 35 O-shaped treats or toys. Seal the sack, and place it somewhere children will discover it.

2. When children locate the sack, act as if you are surprised to find it in the classroom. Encourage children to guess who brought the sack. Point to the number on the sack, and prompt children to say that it is the number of days they have been in school.

3. Draw a vertical line down the center of a piece of chart paper. Write *Yes* above one column and *No* above the other column. Shake the sack, and encourage children to think about what might be inside.

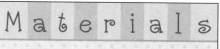

Materials

- Zero's Surprise reproducible (page 49)
- Zero-the-Hero Journals (see page 47)
- paper lunch sack
- O-shaped treats or toys
- chart paper
- transparency/overhead projector
- transparency markers
- crayons or markers

4. Tell children that you will play a guessing game to determine what is inside the sack. Explain that you will ask them a question (e.g., *What is the color?*), and that they should respond with another question (e.g., *Is it red?*).

5. Write the children's question or draw a picture related to it in the "Yes" column if the answer is yes and in the "No" column if the answer is no.

6. Continue until children have asked enough questions to determine what is in the sack. Invite children to name what they think is in the sack.

7. Show children the contents of the sack. Invite children to help you count the items.

8. Make a transparency copy of the Zero-the-Hero's Surprise reproducible, and display it. Show children how to draw a picture of the item at the bottom of the paper. Write *10th* on the first blank line, and write the name of the item on the second blank line. Invite children to draw a picture and copy the number and words on the first blank page in their Zero-the-Hero Journal.

9. Ask children to help you write a sentence about the items in the sack, and write it on the transparency. Encourage children to write their own sentence on their paper.

10. Tell children that Zero-the-Hero will return in ten more days with a new surprise to write about.

Award Tickets

Copy and cut apart this page. Attach one "ticket" to an entry in each child's Zero-the-Hero Journal.

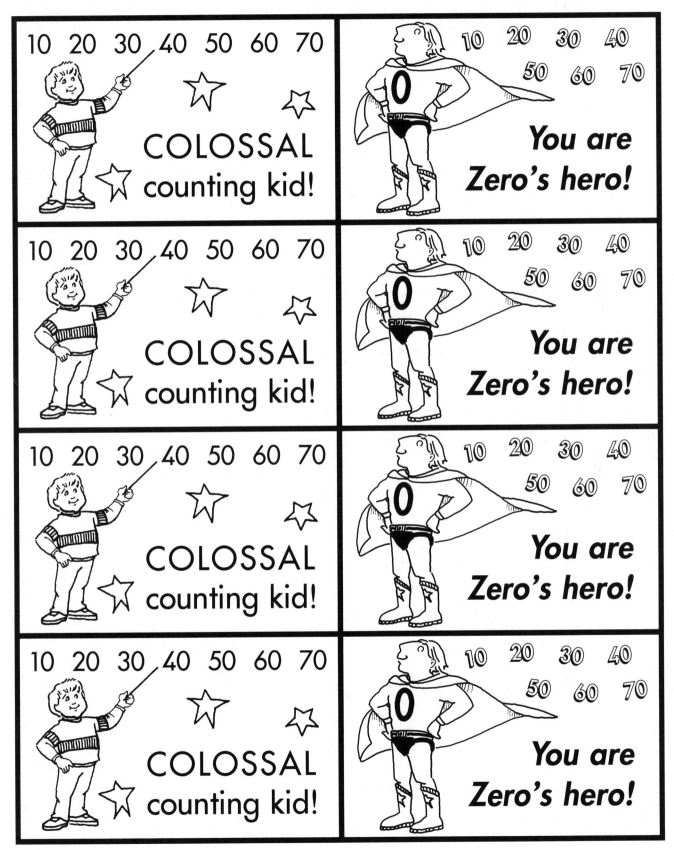

Science

J O U R N A L

Use a digital camera to take a picture of each child. Print the photographs, and give each child the image of himself or herself. Give each child a My Science Journal reproducible and a piece of construction paper. Invite children to cut out the face from their photograph and glue it to the body of the scientist on the reproducible. Have children color their journal reproducible and glue it to their piece of construction paper. Give children several pieces of paper. Help children staple their papers behind their construction paper cover.

Materials

- My Science Journal reproducible (page 53)
- digital camera
- construction paper
- scissors
- glue
- crayons or markers
- lined or unlined paper
- stapler

Have children use their Science Journal to record what they have learned from a science experiment. For example, after a discussion about the changing states of matter, ask children to draw a picture of a snowman and what happens to a snowman when the sun begins to shine. Encourage children to write about their picture.

MY SCIENCE JOURNAL

by _____

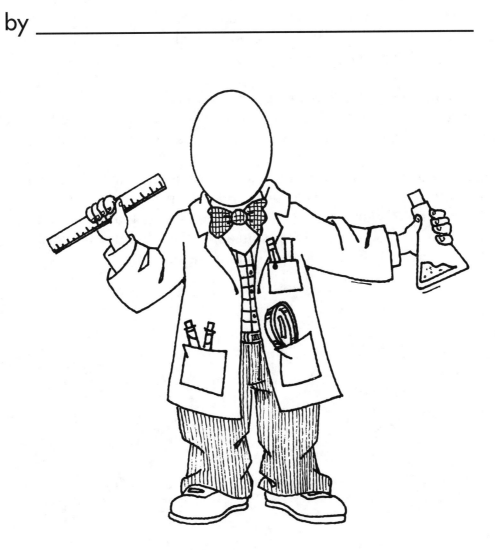

All about Animals

1. Show children how to fold a piece of construction paper in half and then in half again three more times to make 16 identical boxes.

2. Show children the animal book, and tell them that you have been reading this book about animals. Say *I think I would like to write about animals in my journal, so I have folded up this piece of paper, and I will write the name of one animal in each box.*

3. Invite children to name an animal they think might be in the book. Write the name of one animal in each box.

Materials

- Science Journal (page 52)
- 9" x 12" (23 x 30.5 cm) construction paper
- nonfiction book about animals
- scissors
- stapler

4. Cut apart the boxes, and ask children to help you sort them into categories (e.g., pets, zoo animals). Staple together the pages to make a flip book.

5. Tell children you are now ready to write in your Science Journal. Model for children how to write the date at the top of the page, and remind them to begin writing on the left side of the page.

6. Look at the first animal in the book (e.g., an elephant), and say *Today, I will write about elephants in my Science Journal. I will write "Elephants have long trunks."* Demonstrate for children how to write the sentence on a journal page. Continue to model how to write about the same animal, or choose a different animal from the flip book, and write about it.

Award Tickets

Copy and cut apart this page. Attach one "ticket" to an entry in each child's Science Journal.

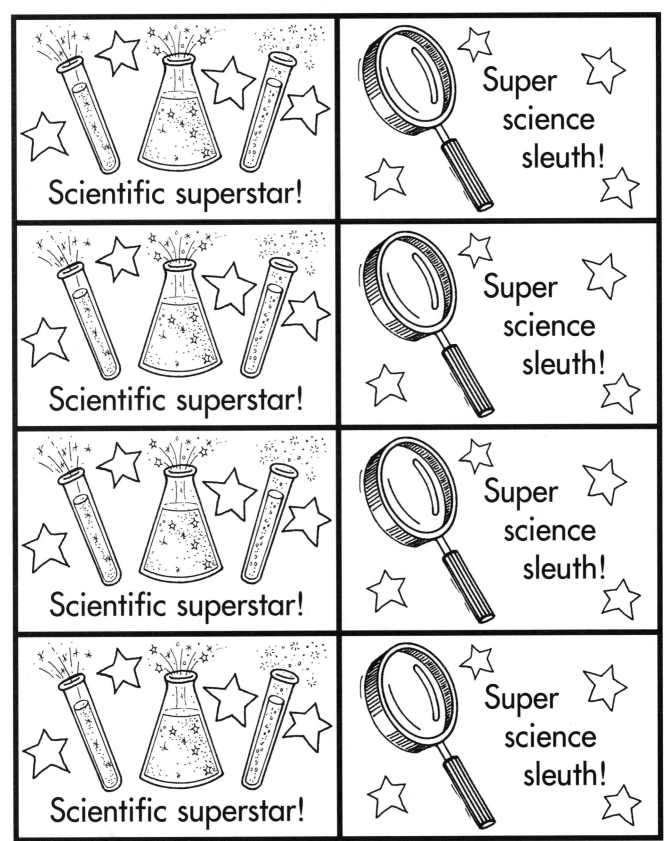

Scientific superstar!

Super science sleuth!

Scientific superstar!

Super science sleuth!

Scientific superstar!

Super science sleuth!

Scientific superstar!

Super science sleuth!

Boo-Boo Binder

J O U R N A L

Use this journal to teach children how to spell the parts of the body and to give them a little attention when they are hurt while at school. Make a copy of the Boo-Boo Binder reproducible, and attach it to the front cover of a three-ring binder. Make several copies of the Boo-Boo reproducible. Hole-punch the copies, and insert them in a binder. Make a copy of the Boo-Boo Binder Word List reproducible, and tape it to the inside front cover of the binder. Place crayons and bandages in a zippered pocket, and insert the pocket into the binder.

Invite children who are injured on the playground or in class to complete a page in the Boo-Boo Binder. Explain that if a child is injured, he or she may draw a picture on a new page in the binder and attach a bandage to the part of his or her body that has been injured. Encourage the child to use the word list on the inside front cover of the binder to help him or her complete a sentence about the injury to go with the drawing.

Boo-Boo Binder

_____'s Boo-Boo

I have a boo-boo on my _____

_____

_____.

Boo-Boo Binder Word List

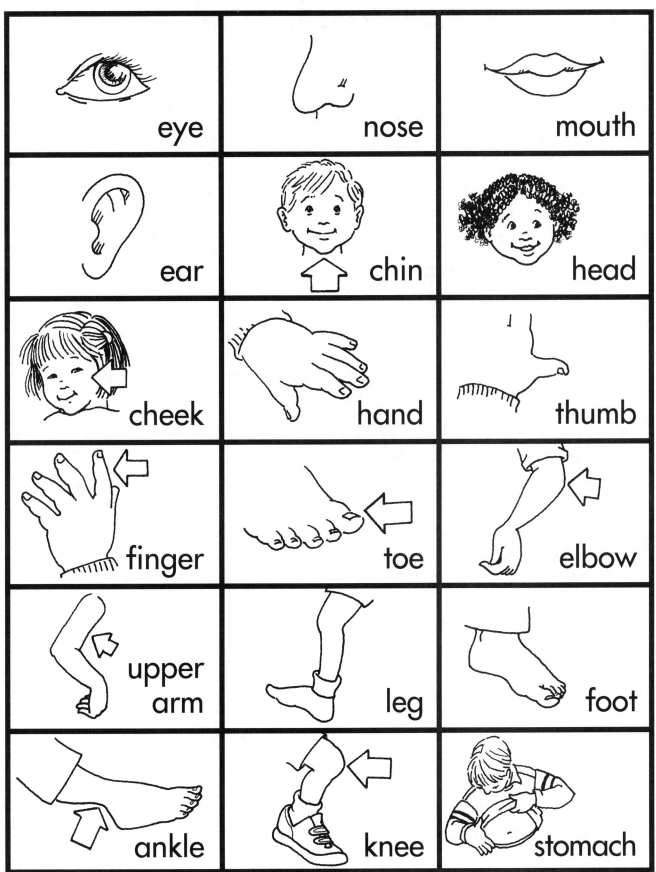

eye

nose

mouth

ear

chin

head

cheek

hand

thumb

finger

toe

elbow

upper arm

leg

foot

ankle

knee

stomach

I Feel Better Now!

1. The first time a child approaches you with a minor injury (and after a health aide has seen the child, if necessary), invite the class to help you help the injured child feel better.

2. Show children the Boo-Boo Binder. Open to the first page, and draw a picture of the child and his or her injury. Model for children how to write the date at the top of the page.

Materials

- Boo-Boo Binder (page 56)

3. Demonstrate for children how to remove a bandage from the zippered pocket, and place it over the injury in the drawing.

4. Flip to the front cover of the binder, and ask children to help you identify the picture of the body part that was injured. Point to the word that accompanies the picture, and write it to complete the sentence below the drawing.

5. Point to the period at the end of your sentence. Remind children that sentences always end with punctuation.

6. Read your sentence aloud to the children. Tell children that if they have a minor injury during the school year they can write about it in this special binder.

Award Tickets

Copy and cut apart this page. Attach one "ticket" to each child's entry in the Boo-Boo Binder.

Bye-bye, boo-boo.

I feel better now!

Bandages make boo-boos better!

Bye-bye, boo-boo.

I feel better now!

Bandages make boo-boos better!

Bye-bye, boo-boo.

I feel better now!

Bandages make boo-boos better!

Bye-bye, boo-boo.

I feel better now!

Bandages make boo-boos better!

Center-Time

JOURNAL

Make several copies of the My Center-Time Journal reproducible, and cut the pages in half to make a cover for each child's journal. Cut several sheets of construction paper and lined or unlined paper in half. Give each child a journal reproducible and half a piece of construction paper. Invite children to color their reproducible and glue it to their construction paper. Give each child several half-sheets of paper, and tell children to place their cover on top. Help children bind their journal.

Materials

- My Center-Time Journal reproducible (page 63)
- scissors
- construction paper
- crayons or markers
- glue
- lined or unlined paper
- bookbinding materials (e.g., stapler or hole punch and curling ribbon)
- sticky notes

Invite children to carry their journal with them as they travel from center to center. Ask children to draw a picture or write a sentence about what they did in the center they just visited. Conference with each child about his or her writing, and on sticky notes record anecdotal notes about their work. Place these notes on the corresponding pages of their journal to help you track children's writing development.

MY CENTER-TIME JOURNAL

by _____

- -

MY CENTER-TIME JOURNAL

by _____

It's All in the Picture

① During the first few weeks of school, take pictures of children working in centers. Glue the photographs to construction paper squares.

② On the back of one of the pictures, write a list of words that are related to the picture.

③ Show children one of the pictures, and say *I took this picture of Megan and Tyler working in the home living center. On the back of the picture, I have made a list of words that I think about when I think of the home living center.* Show children the list of words on the back of the picture, and read them aloud.

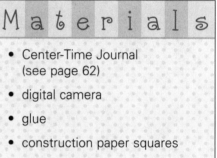

Materials

- Center-Time Journal (see page 62)
- digital camera
- glue
- construction paper squares
- chart paper

④ Rewrite the list (e.g., *food, table, baby, refrigerator*) on a piece of chart paper. Say *Now I want to use this list of words to write about what Megan and Tyler did while working in the home living center in my Center-Time Journal.*

⑤ Repeat this activity over the next several weeks until you have made a list of words for each center. Place these cards at a writing center, and encourage children to use them to write in their Center-Time Journal.

Award Tickets

Copy and cut apart this page. Attach one "ticket" to an entry in each child's Center-Time Journal.

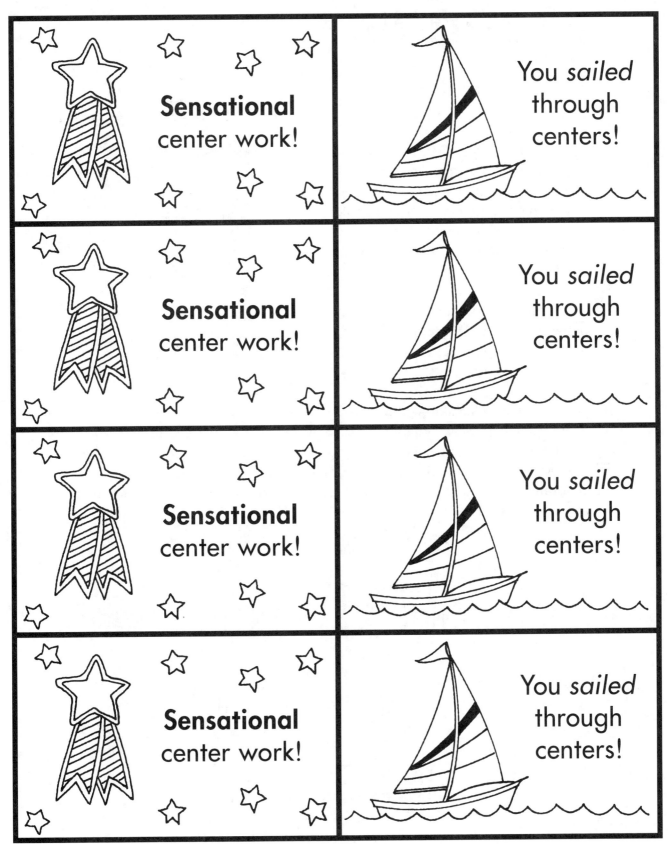

Sensational center work!

You *sailed* through centers!

Monday

J O U R N A L

Make a copy of the My Monday Journal reproducible for each child. Give each child a reproducible and a piece of construction paper. Invite children to color their reproducible and glue it to their piece of construction paper. Give each child 20 pieces of paper to staple behind his or her construction paper cover. Or tell children to glue their construction paper cover to the front of a three-prong folder, and help them hole-punch and insert their papers inside.

Materials

- My Monday Journal reproducible (page 67)
- construction paper
- crayons or markers
- glue
- lined or unlined paper
- stapler or hole punch and three-prong folders
- date stamp

Each Monday, tell children about an event from your weekend. Model for children how to write a journal entry about this event. Invite children to write an event from their weekend in their Monday Journal. Use these Monday Journals as a portfolio to track children's progress. Use a date stamp to help identify children's development as writers over time.

MY MONDAY JOURNAL

by _____

My Own Stories

1 Tell children about something you did or something you learned over the weekend. Draw a picture of the event on a large sheet of construction paper, or show children a photograph. For example, you might tell children that you planted your vegetable garden over the weekend. Tell children all the details of this "adventure," and embellish to pique their interest.

2 Invite children to tell another child about something they did last weekend. Remind children to add as many details as possible.

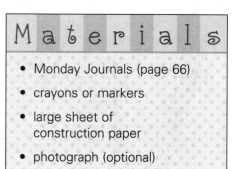

Materials

- Monday Journals (page 66)
- crayons or markers
- large sheet of construction paper
- photograph (optional)

3 Draw a picture of your garden in a Monday Journal. Model for children how to write the date above the picture, and remind them to begin writing on the left side of the page.

4 Tell children you are going to "think through" all of the details of planting your garden again before you write your story. Model for children how to retell the story as you write the sentences below your drawing.

5 Invite children to write about their own weekend adventure in their Monday Journal.

I planted my garden last weekend.

Award Tickets

Copy and cut apart this page. Attach one "ticket" to an entry in each child's Monday Journal.

WILD weekend writer!

Marvelous Monday message!

WILD weekend writer!

Marvelous Monday message!

WILD weekend writer!

Marvelous Monday message!

WILD weekend writer!

Marvelous Monday message!

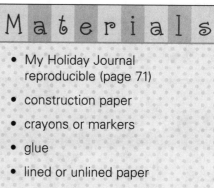

Holiday

J O U R N A L

Give each child a My Holiday Journal reproducible and a piece of construction paper. Invite children to color their reproducible and glue it to their construction paper. Give children several pieces of paper. Help children staple their papers behind their construction paper cover. Or tell children to glue their construction paper cover to the front of a three-prong folder, and help them hole-punch and insert their papers inside the folder.

M a t e r i a l s

- My Holiday Journal reproducible (page 71)
- construction paper
- crayons or markers
- glue
- lined or unlined paper
- stapler or hole punch and three-prong folders

Invite children to write about how people honor particular holidays. Be sure to include special events that are unique to your class or school, such as School Spirit Day or Book Character Day.

MY HOLIDAY JOURNAL

by _____

Holiday "Hoop"la!

1. Place two hula hoops on the ground side by side without overlapping. Write *Valentine's Day* and *Saint Patrick's Day* on separate construction paper cards. Place one card above each hoop. Explain to children that they will use these hoops to help them compare both holidays.

2. Ask children to name words that describe Valentine's Day (e.g., *red*, *cupid*, *heart*), and write them on separate cards. Ask children to name words that describe Saint Patrick's Day (e.g., *green*, *leprechaun*, *shamrock*), and write them on separate cards.

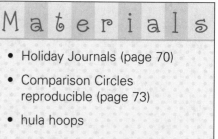

Materials

- Holiday Journals (page 70)
- Comparison Circles reproducible (page 73)
- hula hoops
- construction paper cards
- crayons or markers

3. Combine the cards into a pile. Draw a card from the pile, and read it aloud. Invite a child to place the card in the hoop that corresponds to the holiday the word describes. Continue with new cards and different children until each card has been placed.

4. Read aloud all of the words that are associated with each holiday.

5. Tell children you are going to write a journal entry that shows the difference, or contrast, between Valentine's Day and Saint Patrick's Day. Model for children how to write the date at the top of a page of a Holiday Journal, and remind them to begin writing on the left side of the page.

6. Write *Valentine's Day*. Model for children how to write a sentence to describe a word in the first hoop. For example, write **Red** *is the holiday's color* as you read aloud the sentence. Then write a sentence for a word from the hoop for Saint Patrick's Day.

7. Give each child a Comparison Circles reproducible. Invite children to choose two holidays, and have them draw a picture that is associated with each holiday above separate circles on their diagram. Encourage children to use pictures or real or invented spellings inside the circles to describe each holiday. Then ask children to use their paper to guide them as they write an entry in their Holiday Journal.

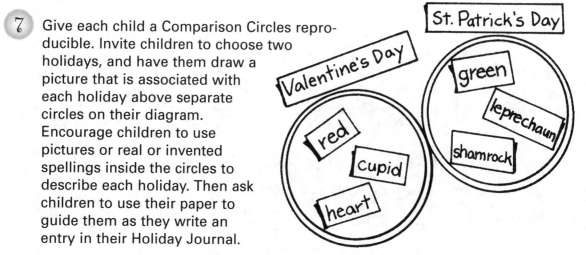

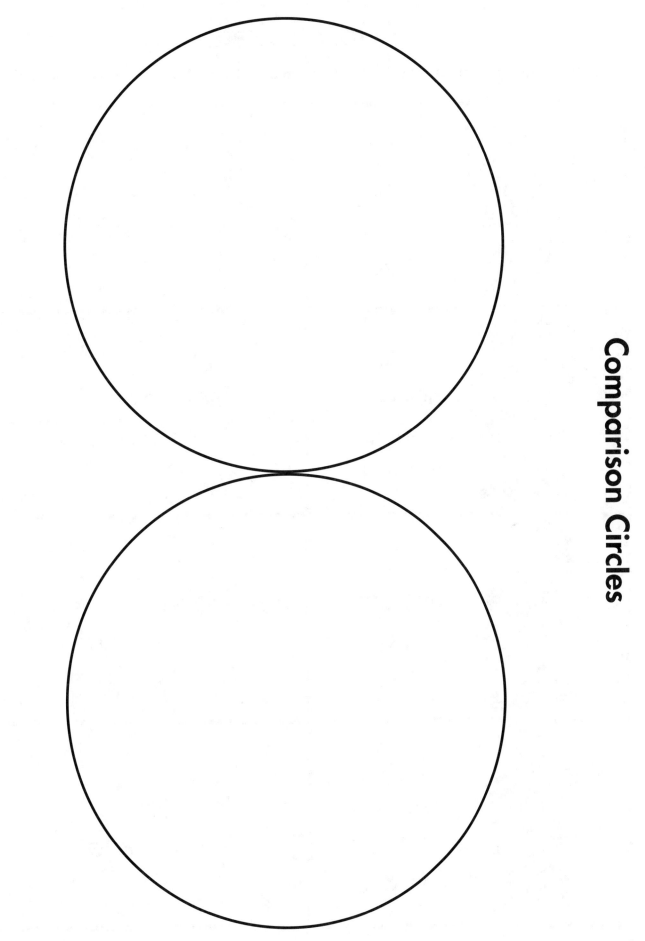

Comparison Circles

Award Tickets

Copy and cut apart this page. Attach one "ticket" to an entry in each child's Holiday Journal.

Monthly

J O U R N A L S

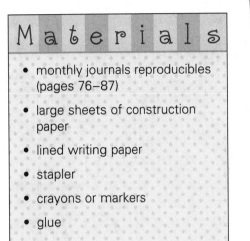

For the current month of the year, choose the corresponding monthly journal reproducible, and make a copy of it for each child in class. Give each child a large sheet of construction paper, and have him or her fold it in half. Give each child 20 pieces of lined writing paper to insert into his or her construction paper cover. Help children staple the papers inside the cover to make a journal. Give each child a copy of the monthly journal reproducible to color and glue to the front of his or her journal.

<table>
<tr><td colspan="2">Materials</td></tr>
<tr><td>•</td><td>monthly journals reproducibles (pages 76–87)</td></tr>
<tr><td>•</td><td>large sheets of construction paper</td></tr>
<tr><td>•</td><td>lined writing paper</td></tr>
<tr><td>•</td><td>stapler</td></tr>
<tr><td>•</td><td>crayons or markers</td></tr>
<tr><td>•</td><td>glue</td></tr>
</table>

Give children a new monthly journal on the first school day of each month. Designate a particular time every day for children to write in their monthly journal. Encourage children to write about the experiences in their life. Remind children to record the date at the top of each new entry.

My
January
Journal

by _____

My February Journal

by _____

My March Journal

by _____

My April Journal

by _____

My May Journal

by _____

by _____

My July Journal

by _____

My August Journal

by _____

by _____

My October Journal

by _____

by _____

by _____

Graphic Organizers Are Always in Season

1　Choose one of the graphic organizers from pages pages 89–100 that correlates with a monthly theme you are teaching (e.g., the apple-and-worms graphic organizer would be suitable for September, when children will create their My September Journal).

2　Enlarge the graphic organizer, and write the main topic (i.e., *Apples*) in the space provided. Identify three subtopics (e.g., apples are different colors; apples are picked in the fall; apples have seeds), and draw a picture for each in the boxes provided. Write a sentence about each picture in the spaces provided.

Materials

- graphic organizers (pages 89–100)
- crayons or markers
- monthly journals

3　Display a monthly journal. Model for children how to write the date at the top of a page, and remind them to begin writing on the left side of the page. Draw a detailed picture in the journal using the ideas from the graphic organizer (e.g., an apple tree with red apples and one with green apples; a person dressed in fall clothes cutting open an apple to expose the seeds). Expand on the sentences from the graphic organizer to write three sentences below the picture.

4　Give each child a copy of the graphic organizer reproducible that relates to the monthly theme you are teaching. Have emergent writers draw pictures, and remind them to begin each sentence with a noun when doing informational writing.

5　Conference with children after they have completed their graphic organizer. Encourage children to add color, size, and shape words to their graphic organizer before they use it to help them write their final entry in their monthly journal.

Topic _____'s

_____

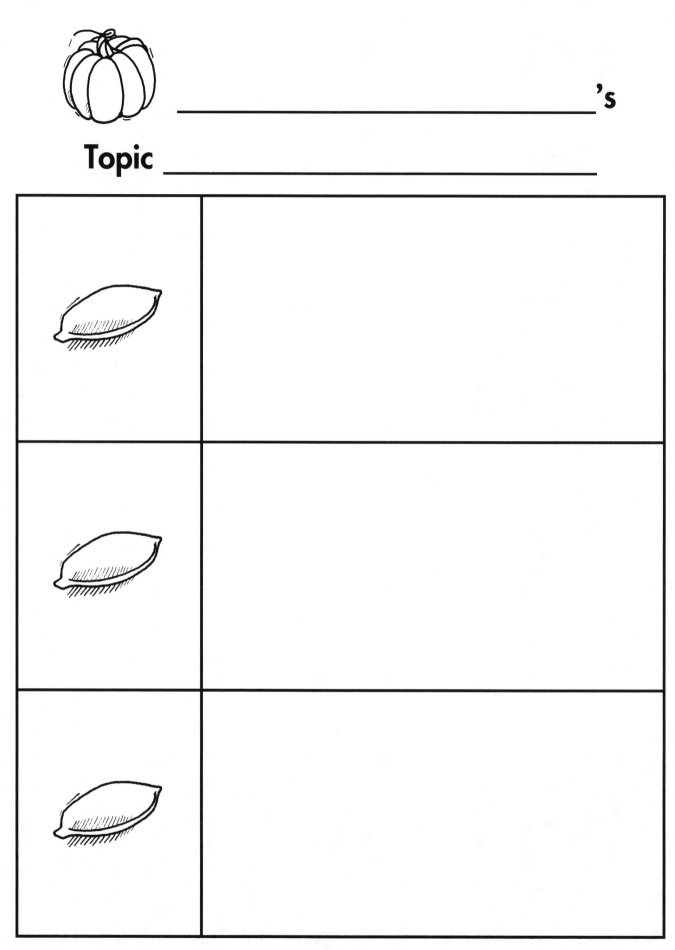

_____'s

Topic _____

 _____'s

Topic _____

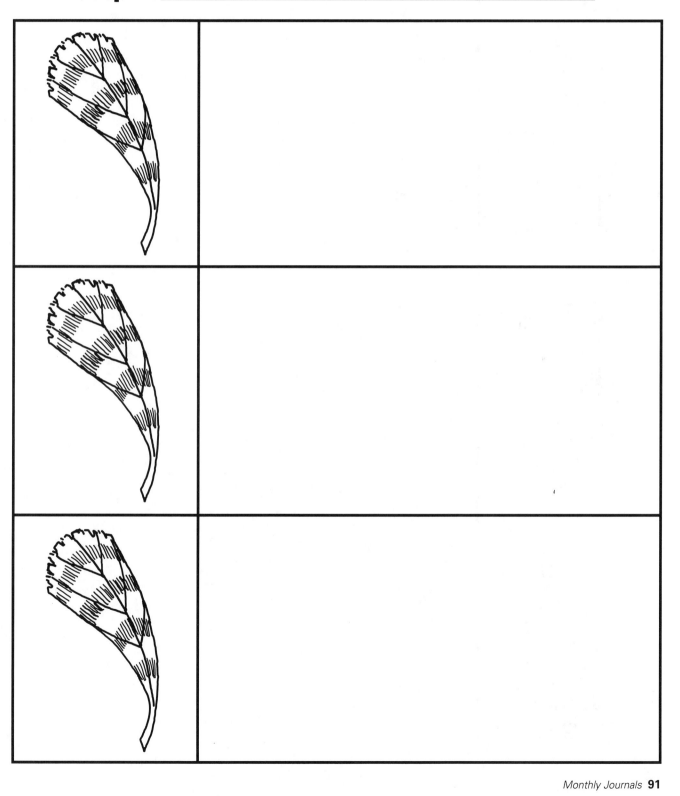

_____'s

Topic _____

_____'s

Topic _____

_____'s

Topic _____

_____'s

Topic _____

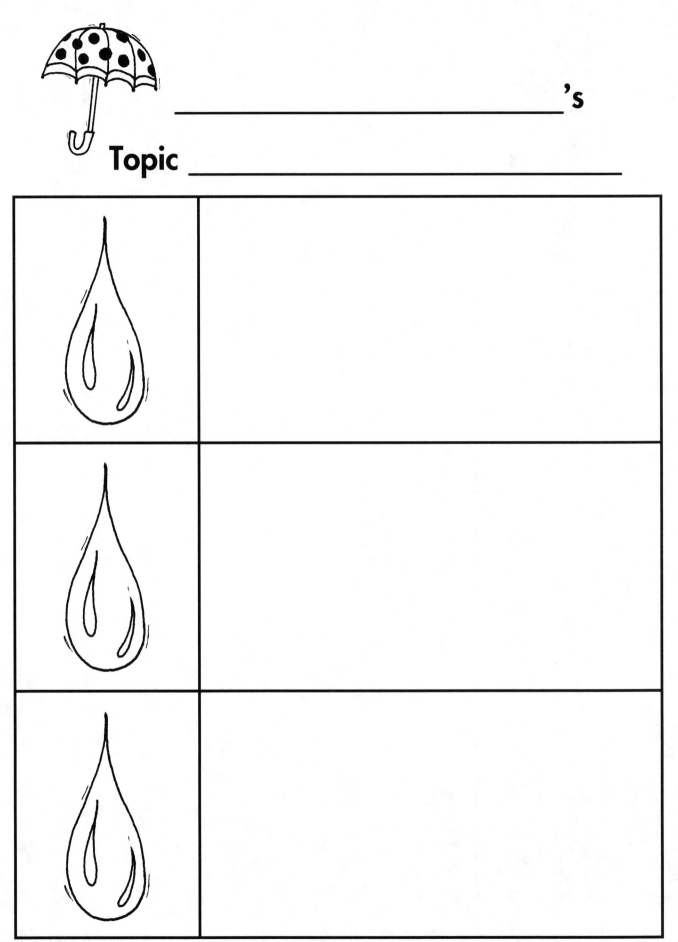

_____'s

Topic _____

_____'s

Topic _____

_____'s

Topic _____

_____'s

Topic _____

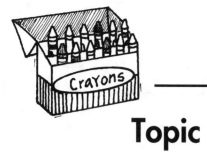 _____'s

Topic _____

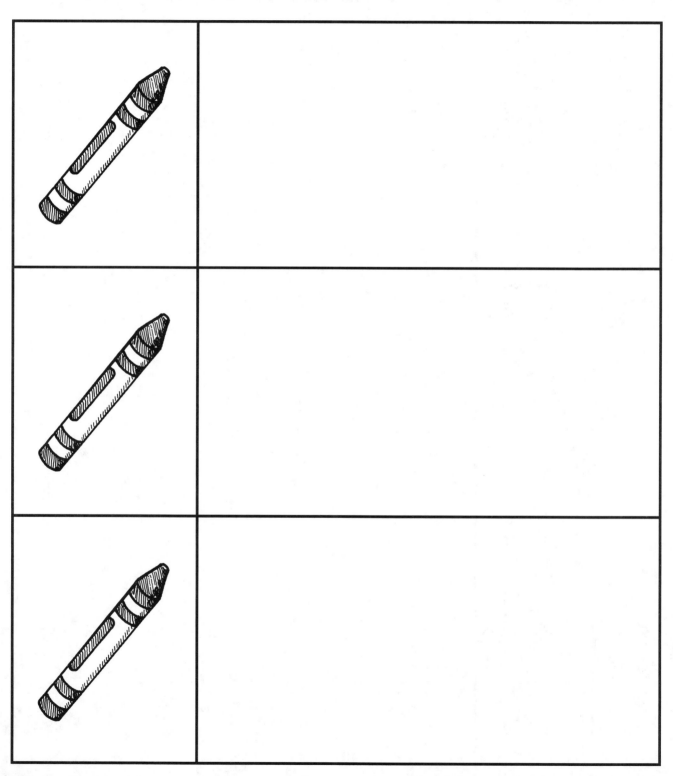

Award Tickets

Copy and cut apart this page. Attach one "ticket" to an entry in each child's monthly journal.

I Don't Know What to Write!

Here are a few ways to answer children's most popular question, What should I write? These activities give children a break from everyday journal writing and inspire them to write fictional stories.

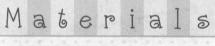

Materials

- My List of Writing Topics reproducible (page 103)

Things I Can Write About

Give each child a My List of Writing Topics reproducible to insert in his or her My Writing Toolbox (see page 7). Encourage children to record on this paper the names of people, places, and things that interest them. Remind children to consult this list whenever they need a topic for a journal entry.

Materials

- Character Cutouts reproducibles (pages 104–105)
- individual class photographs
- scissors
- glue or stapler
- crayons or markers

Character Cutouts

Copy the Character Cutouts reproducibles. Copy and cut apart a class photograph of each child, and glue one onto the face of each character. Cut apart the characters, and give each child the one with his or her face on it. Glue or staple the cutout to a blank page in the child's journal. Encourage children to draw a setting and write a story for their character cutout.

Materials

- sandpaper
- stickers
- small colored pebbles
- blue cellophane
- hay
- tissue paper
- bubble wrap
- cotton
- glue or tape

Art Additions

Choose one of the art materials from the list, or supply one not listed, and glue or tape it to a blank page in a child's journal. Ask children to imagine that the material is part of a story. Encourage children to write the story in their journal.

My List of Writing Topics

People	Places	Things

Character Cutouts

Jumping into Journals © 2006 Creative Teaching Press

Character Cutouts

Conferencing Tips

Consider a conference with a child as an opportunity for a private "minilesson." Work with one child at a time while the other children are writing. Here are some things you might discuss in a conference:

- It is important to hold children accountable for demonstrating the conventions of writing (e.g., spacing, punctuation, and spelling), but you must also reinforce that the true purpose of writing is to convey meaning. A good approach is to focus on only one consistent mistake at a time. A child who is overcorrected tends to write "canned" sentences that are "safe" and easy to write.

- Compare a child's work to that of an author with whom the child is familiar. For example, say *I love how your animals talk just like Eric Carle's did in The Grouchy Ladybug*. Then use the opportunity to introduce speech bubbles and quotation marks to the child.

- Consider the developmental level of the child when you are conferencing. You might limit your suggestions to having the child add more detail to a drawing or using spaces between words. As children progress, ask them to avoid using "I like" to begin a sentence, and encourage them to use descriptive words in their writing.

- Always point out at least one positive aspect of a child's writing before you make a suggestion for improvement. For example, say *You remembered to start each sentence with a capital letter. Very good! Now let me show you something else good writers do.*

- Remind children to use the tools available to them, such as a Traveling Word Wall (see page 7) or a Sound Sheet (see page 8). Also encourage children to reread their stories to make sure they have included adequate information and detail.

Conferencing: Revising Content

Conduct one of these "minilessons" with an individual child. Model for the child one thing he or she could do to make his or her writing easier to read, such as the following:

- Remind the child that we always write from left to right. Show the child a green circle and a red circle cut from construction paper. Ask the child what green and red on a stoplight mean. Open to a page in the child's journal. Have the child place the green circle on the left side of the page and the right circle on the right side of the page. Tell children to use these circles to remember where to begin writing on a page.

- Explain to the child that when you draw a picture, you like to label the things in the picture. Help the child label the things in a picture in the child's journal.

- Demonstrate for the child what to do when writing a word that he or she does not know how to spell. Tell the child you are going to write *Rainbows have different colors.* Say *I write **Rainbows have**, but I do not know how to spell **different**, so I will just write the first letter and ask for help later or look for the word in my Word Wall or Favorite Words folders.*

- Choose a journal entry that does not have very much punctuation. Read the story without pausing. Prompt the child to say that we will need to add some punctuation to let the reader know how to read the story. Help the child read aloud the words and add punctuation where appropriate.

green

I can write from left to right.

red

Conferencing: Expanding Content

The following ideas will help children expand the content of what they are writing:

- Ask a child to read aloud a part of his or her journal entry. Ask *Does this make sense? What could we add to explain things?*
- After a child reads aloud an entire journal entry, ask if there is anything else he or she can add to his or her story. Encourage the child to add adjectives and other descriptors.
- Challenge children to vary the way they begin sentences. Suggest alternatives to beginning with "I like" or "I see."
- Ask a child about the characters in his or her story. Ask *What will your characters do next?*
- Help a child recognize whether or not the events of his or her story follow a logical sequence.

Publishing

On occasion, invite children to "publish" a journal entry for display in the classroom or to send home. Select one of the ideas below to give children's writing a fun, finished look.

Materials

- Publishing Company reproducible (page 111)
- stapler
- construction paper
- stickers
- scissors
- glue

Typed Entry

Ask parent volunteers to type an entry from each child's journal. Invite children to illustrate their work. Staple a construction paper cover to each child's paper, and invite the child to write a title on it. Give children stickers to decorate their cover. Make several copies of the Publishing Company reproducible, and cut apart the individual labels. Give one label to each child. Have children write their name and the year on the blank lines, and have them glue their label to the back of their "book."

Materials

- About the Author reproducible (page 112)
- scissors
- individual class photographs
- glue

About the Author

Make several copies of the About the Author reproducible, and cut apart the individual labels. Give one label to each child. Give each child a small class photograph of himself or herself to glue to the box on their label. Ask children to write about themselves on the blank lines on their label and glue the label to the inside front cover of their "book."

Author: Gavin

Age: 6

Favorite Color: blue

Favorite Place to Go: the playground

Publishing

Materials

- Publishing Company reproducible (page 111)
- scissors
- large sheets of construction paper
- white copy paper
- crayons or markers
- glue

Accordion Book

Invite children to search through their journals for a story that has a definite beginning, middle, and ending. Cut several large sheets of construction paper in half lengthwise, and accordion-fold each piece of paper into three sections to make a "book" for each child. Cut squares of white copy paper, and give three to each child. Tell children to illustrate the beginning, middle, and ending of their story on separate squares. Invite children to write their story beneath their illustrations. Have children glue their squares to their accordion book and fold it up. Ask children to write a title and their name on the front cover. Give each child a label from the Publishing Company reproducible (page 111) to fill out and glue to the back of his or her book.

Materials

- scissors
- paper plates
- metal fasteners
- glue

Paper Plate Books

Make paper plate "books" to publish children's "how to" or "all about me" writing. Show children how to cut a one-fourth wedge from a paper plate. Place this plate on top of a second plate. Insert a metal fastener in the middle of the plates to hold them together. Ask parent volunteers to help you type an entry (divided into four sections) from each child's journal. Help children cut out and glue the first part of their story to the empty space revealed on the bottom plate. Show children how to rotate the top plate to reveal another empty space, and have children glue the next part of their story in that space. Repeat until all four parts of the story have been glued to the bottom plate. Invite children to write a title for their story and their name on the top plate.

Publishing Company

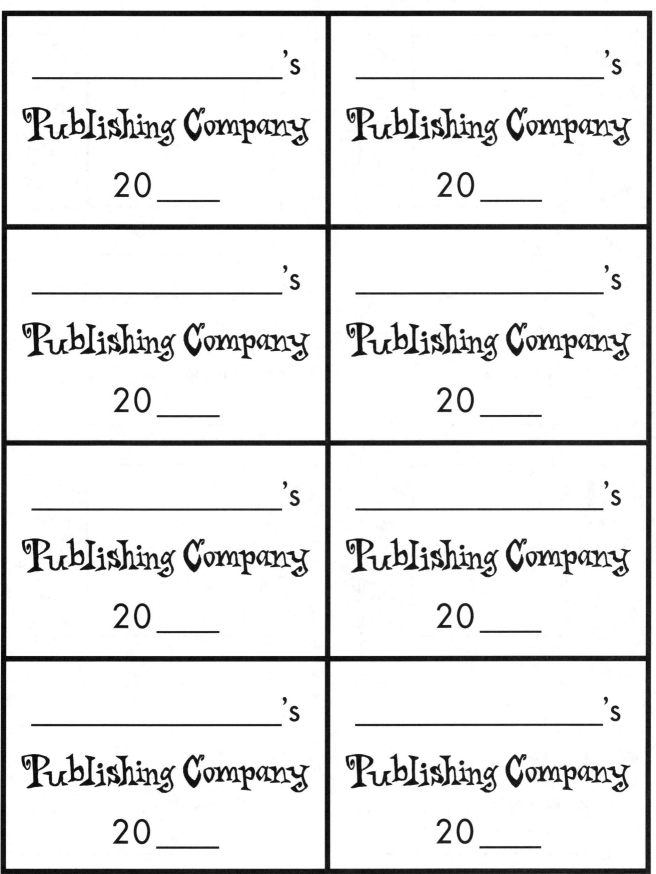

_____'s

Publishing Company

20____

_____'s

Publishing Company

20____

_____'s

Publishing Company

20____

_____'s

Publishing Company

20____

_____'s

Publishing Company

20____

_____'s

Publishing Company

20____

_____'s

Publishing Company

20____

_____'s

Publishing Company

20____

About the Author

Author: _____

Age: _____

Favorite Color: _____

Favorite Place to Go: _____

_____

Author: _____

Age: _____

Favorite Color: _____

Favorite Place to Go: _____

_____

Author: _____

Age: _____

Favorite Color: _____

Favorite Place to Go: _____

_____

Author: _____

Age: _____

Favorite Color: _____

Favorite Place to Go: _____

_____

Jumping into Journals © 2006 Creative Teaching Press